W9-BGQ-771

LETTERS TO TIMOTHY

DISCIPLESHIP IN ACTION

13 Studies for Individuals or Groups

MARGARET FROMER & SHARREL KEYES

Harold Shaw Publishers • Wheaton, Illinois

ISBN 0-87788-490-0

Cover photo © 1994 by Mike Marshall

99   98   97   96   95   94

10   9   8   7   6   5   4

CONTENTS

INTRODUCTION

Many scholars believe that after Paul was released from his Roman "house arrest" (described in the last chapter of Acts) he went on one last missionary journey. Paul left Timothy in charge of a young congregation in Ephesus while he continued west.

The church at Ephesus had serious problems: it was being influenced by false teachers who denied the resurrection of Christ, who urged a false asceticism by suggesting that those who remained celibate and refrained from eating meat were spiritually superior, and whose teaching was involved with cultural myths, superstitions, and pointless genealogies. They just didn't seem to understand the clear facts of the gospel. As if that weren't enough, the church was facing some internal problems: how to keep order, who should be chosen for offices of responsibility, and how to meet the needs of individual members of the congregation.

Timothy, apparently, needed a lot of encouragement. Although he had been Paul's ministry companion for about fifteen years and was his spiritual "son," Paul sensed Timothy was unsure of himself. Consequently, both letters are full of encouragement for confidence-building.

The second letter takes on a more personal note. Paul has again been imprisoned in Rome, but this time in chains, in a dungeon, waiting for a sentence of death to be carried out. He prepares Timothy to carry on without him and helps him understand how to face his responsibilities.

How does all this apply to your Bible study group? The person who is wondering just how seriously he should take Scripture will get some help as Paul talks about the importance of right doctrine and "sound words." And we could all pick up some pointers on how to discern and react to false teachers and teaching. Many people have questions about prayer and corporate worship: Paul lays down some guidelines. The list of requirements for officeholders will not only help a nominating committee, but can help each of us set specific goals for personal maturity.

As we studied these two letters, what stood out most to us was Paul's care and love for Timothy. We learned a lot about how to build up another member of the household of God, how to pray for that person, and how to encourage him toward the maturity and fulfillment that God has for him. In looking back over our own spiritual pilgrimages, we could see that the people who had helped us most had, like Paul in his relationship to Timothy, encouraged us to depend on God and to have the confidence that God could meet all our needs. We hope to follow these "Paul-Timothy" examples in our own lives and relationships.

When you read Paul's letters to Timothy, allow them to be God's letters to you. Soak them up as you would words from a trusted friend. Determine that you will live out the principles and instructions that will enable you to live the life that is "life indeed."

Margaret Fromer and Sharrel Keyes

HOW TO USE THIS STUDYGUIDE

Fisherman studyguides are based on the inductive approach to Bible study. Inductive study is discovery study; we discover what the Bible says as we ask questions about its content and search for answers. This is quite different from the process in which a teacher *tells* a group *about* the Bible and what it means and what to do about it. In inductive study God speaks directly to each of us through his Word.

A group functions best when a leader keeps the discussion on target, but this leader is neither the teacher nor the "answer person." A leader's responsibility is to *ask*—not *tell*. The answers come from the text itself as group members examine, discuss, and think together about the passage.

There are four kinds of questions in each study. The first is an *approach question*. Used before the Bible passage is read, this question breaks the ice and helps you focus on the topic of the Bible study. It begins to reveal where thoughts and feelings need to be transformed by Scripture.

Some of the earlier questions in each study are *observation questions* designed to help you find out basic facts—who, what, where, when, and how.

When you know what the Bible says you need to ask, *What does it mean?* These *interpretation questions* help you to discover the writer's basic message.

Application questions ask, *What does it mean to me?* They challenge you to live out the Scripture's life-transforming message.

Fisherman studyguides provide spaces between questions for jotting down responses and related questions you would like to raise in the group. Each group member should have a copy of the studyguide and may take a turn in leading the group.

A group should use any accurate, modern translation of the Bible such as the *New International Version,* the *New American Standard Bible,* the *Revised Standard Version,* the *New Jerusalem Bible,* or the *Good News Bible.* (Other translations or paraphrases of the Bible may be referred to when additional help is needed.) Bible commentaries should not be brought to a Bible study because they tend to dampen discussion and keep people from thinking for themselves.

SUGGESTIONS FOR GROUP LEADERS

1. Read and study the Bible passage thoroughly beforehand, grasping its themes and applying its teachings for yourself. Pray that the Holy Spirit will "guide you into truth" so that your leadership will guide others.

2. If the studyguide's questions ever seem ambiguous or unnatural to you, rephrase them, feeling free to add others that seem necessary to bring out the meaning of a verse.

3. Begin (and end) the study promptly. Start by asking someone to pray for God's help. Remember, the Holy Spirit is the teacher, not you!

4. Ask for volunteers to read the passages out loud.

5. As you ask the studyguide's questions in sequence, encourage everyone to participate in the discussion. If some are silent, ask "What do you think, Heather?" or, "Dan, what can you add to tha answer?" or suggest, "Let's have an answer from someone who hasn't spoken up yet."

6. If a question comes up that you can't answer, don't be afraid to admit that you're baffled! Assign the topic as a research project for someone to report on next week.

7. Keep the discussion moving and focused. Though tangents will inevitably be introduced, you can bring the discussion back to the topic at hand. Learn to pace the discussion so that you finish a study each session you meet.

8. Don't be afraid of silences: some questions take time to answer and some people need time to gather courage to speak. If silence persists, rephrase your question, but resist the temptation to answer it yourself.

9. If someone comes up with an answer that is clearly illogical or unbiblical, ask him or her for further clarification: "What verse suggests that to you?"

10. Discourage Bible-hopping and overuse of cross-references. Learn all you can from *this* passage, along with a few important references suggested in the studyguide.

11. Some questions are marked with a ♦. This indicates that further information is available in the Leader's Notes at the back of the guide.

12. For further information on getting a new Bible study group started and keeping it functioning effectively, read Gladys Hunt's *You Can Start a Bible Study Group* and *Pilgrims in Progress: Growing through Groups* by Jim and Carol Plueddemann.

SUGGESTIONS FOR GROUP MEMBERS

1. Learn and apply the following ground rules for effective Bible study. (If new members join the group later, review these guidelines with the whole group.)

2. Remember that your goal is to learn all that you can *from the Bible passage being studied.* Let it speak for itself without using Bible commentaries or other Bible passages. There is more than enough in each assigned passage to keep your group productively occupied for one session. Sticking to the passage saves the group from insecurity and confusion.

3. Avoid the temptation to bring up those fascinating tangents that don't really grow out of the passage you are discussing. If the topic is of common interest, you can bring it up later in informal conversation following the study. Meanwhile, help each other stick to the subject!

4. Encourage each other to participate. People remember best what they discover and verbalize for themselves. Some people are naturally shyer than others, or they may be afraid of making a mistake. If your discussion is free and friendly and you show real interest in what other group members think and feel, they will be more likely to speak up. Remember, the more people involved in a discussion, the richer it will be.

5. Guard yourself from answering too many questions or talking too much. Give others a chance to express themselves. If you are one who participates easily, discipline yourself by counting to ten before you open your mouth!

6. Make personal, honest applications and commit yourself to letting God's Word change you.

HOW DO WE KNOW WHEN WE'RE TRUE TO THE TRUTH?

1 Timothy 1:1-11

We live in an age of relativity. Insisting anything is right or true earns at least a raised eyebrow from hearers who believe that each person's preference is as true for him as a word from God. Yet God's authority has always been under fire. It was challenged in Timothy's day by the followers of other gods, and it is challenged today by those who deny spiritual realities altogether. Paul begins this first letter to Timothy by commanding him to adhere to the truth God has revealed through Jesus Christ. This would not be an easy job in the diverse religious climate of Ephesus, where Timothy offered leadership to a young congregation.

1. What kinds of influence—both negative and positive— have you had on the faith of other people?

Read 1 Timothy 1:1-7.

    2. What assignment does Paul give Timothy?

◆ **3.** What different kinds of objections does Paul have to these men as teachers?

    How, by contrast, does Paul describe his own teaching?

    4. How can you use Paul's instructions to Timothy to evaluate a teacher of God's Word?

5. Paul says these false teachers make two basic mistakes in what they are teaching (verses 3-7): Where do they get their doctrine? What's wrong with their teaching?

Read 1 Timothy 1:8-11.

6. To whom does the law communicate God's principles of living?

7. Why do those who have accepted sound doctrine not need the law?

8. Why do sound doctrine and law not conflict?

9. How should each be used?

10. Why is Paul so careful to insist that teachers have both sound character and sound doctrine? (Refer to the whole passage for your answers.)

11. What does Paul mean when he says he has been "entrusted" (verse 11) with the gospel?

♦ **12.** In what way(s) have you been entrusted with the gospel?

13. How can you tell when you are doing a good job in carrying out this trust?

14. What encouragements does this passage have for you, as you act responsibly with this gospel?

HOW DOES GOD EQUIP US FOR SERVICE?

1 Timothy 1:12-20

Often our very deficiencies or failures can later help us make a contribution to others. The person with a history of abuse is more able to help other victims. A former gang member, corporate swindler, or drug offender knows the excuses and pitfalls that go with these lifestyles, and so can shrewdly present God's grace and truth to those people. God has a long history of turning the bad around to bring about good. There's no better example of this than the life of the apostle Paul.

1. Describe a time when God turned a "weakness" into strength in your life or the life of someone you know.

Read 1 Timothy 1:12-20.

2. In view of his past record, how would it seem obvious that Paul was not fitted to serve Jesus Christ?

3. To what advantage did God turn Paul's negative qualities?

4. How is God's patience shown in the passage?

5. Under what circumstances would it be helpful for you to remember how patient God is?

6. Sometimes our basic character traits get out of hand and cause us a lot of trouble. These same characteristics, in God's hands, can become our strongest assets. Write down what you consider to be two or three of your weakest points. Share one with the group.

What elements within that character trait could God redirect so that the results would be positive instead of negative?

What is your part in helping God make this particular change?

7. What provisions had God made for strengthening Timothy?

♦ **8.** What can we expect from the active combination of faith and conscience? (See also verses 3-7.)

9. From the entire chapter of 1 Timothy 1, what were the various ways God had equipped Paul and Timothy for the job he had given them?

10. Look at the responsibilities God has given you. What are some particular ways he has equipped you for his service?

11. Give God thanks and praise in your own words, using Paul's praise as a model.

HOW CAN WE LIVE A TRANQUIL LIFE?

1 Timothy 2

Who doesn't want peace? Who doesn't long for a sense of order? But it is hard to come by. In a culture that values competition and self-development, it is difficult to model God's goodness and self-lessness. Paul urges us to challenge our society's assumptions in practical ways. He gives Timothy some advice that remains valuable to us today.

1. What gives you peace? How much does it depend on you, and how much on outside sources?

Read 1 Timothy 2:1-7.

2. In a community that includes Christians and non-Christians, what does God want to see happening (verses 1- 4)?

3. What did God do to implement his desires (verses 5-7)?

4. Why was it necessary for God to provide a "mediator," a "ransom," a "testimony," and a "teacher"?

5. How can knowing God's desire (verse 4) affect our prayer life?

♦ **6.** Think of two individuals on a local level and two on a national or international level for whom you should pray. For each one, write down a specific request or reason for thanksgiving.

Pray sentence prayers in your group.

Read 1 Timothy 2:8-15.

7. What sort of problems do you think Paul was trying to solve by giving these specific instructions?

♦ **8.** How are women supposed to adorn themselves? In what ways would this enhance a woman's beauty? Why?

How would adorning themselves in this manner contribute to the well-being of the whole group?

9. In what areas in your church or neighborhood could you or your group give of yourselves in good deeds?

♦ **10.** What are the scriptural principles upon which Paul based his instructions to women?

How does his quote from Genesis add weight to his explanation?

11. How do Paul's instructions to men and women in this chapter promote the life he described in verse 2? (Use the whole chapter.)

12. What would you be doing differently if you followed the instructions of this chapter?

13. From which of these instructions could your church benefit most right now?

How can you help bring about this change?

WHAT ARE REQUIREMENTS FOR LEADERS IN GOD'S HOUSEHOLD?

1 Timothy 3

Often leadership goes to those who have power or money. Positions are acquired through political scheming and "connections." God has been showing us that it is important to have good *character*. His Old Testament prophets spoke out against evil rulers and dishonest priests. True leadership comes through example, integrity, and love for God and people.

1. Describe someone who, in your opinion, has good leadership qualities.

Read 1 Timothy 3:1-13.

♦ **2.** As you look at the lists of requirements for overseers and deacons, what descriptive words do you see that indicate the level of excellence required?

3. What are the dangers involved in these offices?

4. What relationship do you see between the seriousness of the job and the specific requirements mentioned?

5. How could this kind of church leadership be helpful to you personally right now?

6. If you were to aspire to one of these offices, how would you prepare yourself?

♦ **7.** How can a church help its members be ready for these offices?

How can we know when people *are* ready?

8. How can a church develop leaders of this caliber?

9. If you are married, how can you help your spouse prepare for a job like this? Similarly, how can you help a
friend be ready to take on that responsibility?

Read 1 Timothy 3:14-16.

10. What case does Paul make for the importance of the
church?

11. How do you need to change your behavior in order to
fit better into God's household?

♦ **12.** Pray now for the leaders in your church and for your relationship to them. Pray for them briefly, specifically, and by name.

HOW CAN I BE A GOOD DISCIPLE?

1 Timothy 4

We all need help and encouragement to grow in our faith, and Timothy was no exception. As a young leader Timothy faced many pitfalls and difficulties in ministering to his church. Paul urges him to persevere, warning Timothy of some of the dangers of the spiritual battle Christians face, and offering effective ways to use his gifts faithfully.

1. Think of someone who has helped you grow spiritually. What made their influence significant?

Read 1 Timothy 4:1-5.

♦ **2.** What are the dangers presented in verses 1-5?

3. What negative attitudes toward life are expressed in these verses?

4. How might an attitude of thanksgiving help you remain unmoved by such false teaching?

Read 1 Timothy 4:6-10.

5. What do you feel like doing when you hear what seems to you a silly myth? *laughing*

What does Paul suggest doing?

Having godliness as a goal

♦ **6.** What incentives are suggested for training yourself in godliness? *eternal life*

Read 1 Timothy 4:11-16.

7. If you feel unequal to the job God has given you, what should you do about it?

8. In what different areas should Christians exercise discipline?

9. What are God's instructions for growing in spiritual maturity and leading others to do the same?

10. Pauls says to watch our doctrine closely. How do we resist false doctrine and teachings?

11. In what one way can you begin to train yourself in godliness so that you will be resistant to wrong doctrines?

HOW ARE CHRISTIANS TO CARE FOR ONE ANOTHER?

1 Timothy 5:1-16

We will always be surrounded by people with great needs. Even Jesus said that the poor would always be with us. The book of James warns us not to ignore physical and practical needs while trying to minister to people's spiritual needs. But where do we begin? And where do we say, "I can't do anymore?" Paul offers sound guidelines in a specific situation that called for much discernment and love.

1. Recall a time when someone helped you when you truly needed it. What made their assistance so effective?

Read 1 Timothy 5:1-8.

2. Name the various groups within the Christian community with which Timothy is going to have to deal.

3. What words describe the attitude Timothy should have toward these different groups of people?

◆ **4.** Who are the various people responsible for a widow's welfare?

5. What does Paul say about family responsibilities?

Read 1 Timothy 5:9-16.

6. If you anticipated ever enrolling on the widow's list, what would you need to be doing now in order to qualify?

7. What responsibilities did these widows have?

8. What needs does your church or community have that could be met by women of this caliber?

9. How does Paul show understanding and thoughtfulness for younger widows?

37

10. What are some practical safeguards against the temptations Paul mentions? (Apply to men as well as women as it is appropriate to your group.)

♦ **11.** What are some of a widow's problems in our society?

12. Think of two widows you know: one in your family, one unrelated. In what practical ways might you or your church help these women?

HOW AM I MY BROTHER'S KEEPER?

Timothy 5:17–6:2

We cannot do anything to earn God's love. But when we have responded to his love by trusting Christ, we enter into partnership with God. His love transforms us. And his love works through us to change others. This means that Christians must be accountable to one another in the Lord. This involves helping each other to grow and to steer clear of sinful patterns. Not a popular concept. But Paul knew the devastation that could occur when Christians, and particularly their leaders, did not look after one another.

1. When has someone else's leadership seemed intrusive to you? When has it saved you from making mistakes or falling into sin?

Read 1 Timothy 5:17-22.

2. What are Timothy's responsibilities toward elders?

Why is each of these commands important?

3. What temptations does Timothy face in regard to elders? In each case, what would be some possible harmful results?

4. What are some of the advantages of quickly involving a new Christian (or new group member) in Christian responsibilities?

5. What disadvantages does this passage suggest that there are in giving responsibility too early?

What other disadvantages can you think of?

♦ **6.** How can you help the new person feel that he or she is a contributing member without being "hasty in the laying on of hands?"

7. What are some ways we might "share in the sins of others"?

Read 1 Timothy 5:23–6:2.

8. Paul's exhortation of verse 23 doesn't seem "spiritual" in nature; what does it have to do with involvement in another's growth as a Christian?

9. What do you think Paul is trying to tell Timothy in verses 24-25? In what ways, if any, are our spiritual leaders responsible for our participation in sin?

10. What instructions in this chapter can help a leader watch over growing Christians and help them avoid or get out of sinful lifestyles?

11. What are some potential problems for the Christian slaves?

What were some potential problems for the Christian masters?

12. What might be a close equivalent today of the slave-master relationship, and how can we apply Paul's words to these situations?

13. What does this passage teach that, if followed, would allow you to live more comfortably with your family? With your Christian community?

WHAT'S SO GOOD ABOUT THE GOOD LIFE?

1 Timothy 6:3-21

We are drawn to God for many different reasons, not all of them noble. Some people, when they discover that the Christian life involves a cost, wander off to the next system promising the "good life." Others attempt to use religion to help them achieve the same selfish ends they've always aimed for. Often, a "new" religion—and Christianity was new when Paul wrote this letter to Timothy—attracts the very people who have been too rebellious to settle into any of the existing systems. However, Paul makes it clear that for those who truly take hold of Christ, the satisfactions are well worth the cost.

1. How has being a Christian benefited you (include areas other than spiritual)?

Read 1 Timothy 6:3-10.

♦ **2.** Several times in the course of his letter Paul has
warned Timothy about men whose teaching does not
agree with the gospel. Read these passages: 1 Timothy
1:3-7, 19-20; 4:1-5, 7.

What is characteristic of a) their teaching and b) them as
teachers?

Reference	Teaching	Teachers
1:3-7		
1:19-20		
4:1-5		
4:7		

From *today's* passage, what does Paul add to his descrip-
tion of these men and their teaching?

♦ **3.** What are the characteristics of those who follow these false teachings?

4. What are the goals of these false teachers?

5. What might both the false teachers and their followers gain by getting involved in "religion"?

6. Are there ways you use religion to satisfy your own ends?

7. What are the dangers of wanting to be both religious and rich?

Read 1 Timothy 6:11-21.

8. How would these instructions help Timothy to avoid using his spiritual position for personal gain (verses 11-16, 20-21)?

9. Why would Paul's exhortation in verses 13-16 add force to his instructions?

10. What specific steps can you take to avoid the problems that your possessions might cause you?

11. Verse 6 indicates that there are legitimate profits for you in a godly life. What are they?

12. From the instructions in this chapter, what do you need to change in order to experience more fully the benefits that God has promised?

WHAT REASON DO WE HAVE TO BE CONFIDENT?

2 Timothy 1

It's difficult enough to walk securely when bad things happen to us and those we love. But when we are living in a way that sets us apart from the rest of the world, maintaining confidence becomes a work of sheer grace. By the time Paul wrote this letter, which scholars believe to be his last before his death, he had learned much about keeping perspective in a world that is no longer home for the Christian. He had learned firsthand that Jesus Christ is the one in whom we can have the fullest confidence.

1. When has it been hardest for you to be a Christian?

Read 2 Timothy 1.

◆ **2.** What came to Paul's mind when he remembered Timothy?

3. What reasons did Paul have for encouraging Timothy to revive his gift (verses 6-7)?

4. What do you think Timothy's gift might have been, in view of the instructions Paul gave him?

5. Under the circumstances Paul described, of what might he and Timothy have been ashamed (verse 8)?

6. How would knowing about the actions of the men in verses 15-18 have helped Timothy not be ashamed of Paul and the gospel?

7. What are the reasons Paul told Timothy not to be ashamed?

♦ **8.** If you wish, share with the group a time when you, as a Christian, have felt fear or shame.

9. Why was Paul so confident in his faith?

10. Referring to what Paul said in this passage, how would you explain to someone who does not yet know Christ what is involved in God's promise of life?

11. Paul is reminding Timothy of these facts to help him get back the confidence and zest he once had. Which of these facts do you need to remember?

12. Think of one thing you would have done differently today (or this week) if you could have had this kind of confidence. Share it with the group.

13. As you think through the rest of your week, what specific steps can you take to use the power, love, and self-discipline that God offers you in the Spirit?

WHAT ARE MY GOALS?

2 Timothy 2:1-19

Most of us have heard the saying: "Aim at nothing and you'll hit it every time." Although we can accomplish good work and growth only by means of grace through Jesus Christ, we must participate and be responsible through our own hard work, intelligence, and gifts. The Christian's life and work make up a wonderful partnership with God, who created us in his image.

1. What goals do you have for your life this year?

Read 2 Timothy 2:1-13.

2. What different aspects of ministry did Paul foresee for
for which Timothy would need strength? (Refer also to
2 Timothy 1:13-14.)

3. How is being strong in grace different from gritting
your teeth and carrying on?

GODS
RICHES
AT
CHRISTS
EXPENSE

How do you go about strengthening yourself inwardly?

4. What jobs do you have for which you need more than
your own strength?

5. What type of competence was Timothy to look for in the people he entrusted with his teachings?

♦ **6.** Using the chart below, note the metaphors (figurative pictures) Paul used in this passage, how each shed light on what Timothy's work would involve, and what would result. Discuss.

Metaphor	What his work will involve	Results promised

7. How did Paul reinforce and illustrate his teaching with practical experiences that nothing worthwhile is ever easy (verses 8-13)?

Read 2 Timothy 2:14-19.

8. What two types of workmen are described in this paragraph? By what actions are they known?

9. How have you observed that quarrels about words are hard on those who hear them?

10. What are the results of good or bad teaching?

11. Review your actions and attitudes while you were at your workplace this past week. Describe the kind of "workman" you are.

12. What goals can this passage help you set so that you will be able to present yourself to God as "one approved"?

HOW CAN WE HANDLE TIMES OF STRESS?

2 Timothy 2:20–3:17

Psychologists speak of "good" stress and "bad" stress. Good stress gives us the incentive to move forward, to solve our problems, and resolve conflicts. Bad stress is destructive to us mentally, emotionally, and physically, if we don't find a way to eliminate or control it.

We can avoid some stress; the sort that comes through our fascination with destructive people. We can patiently resolve other forms of stress, such as the kind that buffets us when we must disagree with influential people so the truth can triumph. Paul's experience, related briefly at the end of 2 Timothy 3, is a good example of surviving the bad and using the good.

1. What stresses most affect your spiritual life and growth?

Read 2 Timothy 2:20-26.

2. What attitudes and practices was Timothy supposed to cultivate?

3. How did Paul's analogy of the vessels help explain his instructions to Timothy?

4. What impulses of youth, referred to in verse 22, would be a hindrance to usefulness to the Lord?

5. Why was Timothy to be gentle with his opponents?

6. How should a Christian handle quarrelsome opponents?

Can you share a situation you are presently concerned about, in which you need to apply Paul's instructions?

Read 2 Timothy 3:1-9.

7. What are some human motives that contribute to times of stress?

8. What was to be Timothy's response to the people described here?

♦ **9.** Why do you suppose his response to these people was to be different from his response to the group we saw previously in 2:25-26?

10. What might have been the danger in trying to witness to these particular people?

11. What do you learn from these passages about the importance of the company you keep?

How has the right company helped you become a "useful vessel"?

Read 2 Timothy 3:10-17.

12. Look at Paul's list of life characteristics, especially in verse 10. Describe how someone else has been a good example to you in one of these areas.

13. What did Paul offer Timothy to enable him to stand in times of stress (verses 14-16)? How would Scripture be a help?

14. What does a person need to do in order to be complete and equipped for God's work? (Use all of today's material.)

HOW CAN WE KEEP GOING?

2 Timothy 4

We are used to thinking of Paul as super-human—easy to admire but more difficult to like. It is hard to believe he ever felt lonely, discouraged, or afraid. In this chapter, however, it is easy to see his humanity. He confers his commission on Timothy, his "son in the faith," and shares his love, his hurt, and his longing in these final, moving words.

1. Describe a person whose life has been an inspiration to you, especially during times of difficult growth and change.

Read 2 Timothy 4.

2. In what different ways did Paul strengthen his appeal to Timothy to preach the gospel?

3. What phrases did Paul use to describe Jesus Christ (verse 1)?

How would you feel if you were given a commission in the presence of a person like this?

4. Summarize Paul's charge to Timothy in this chapter.

5. In what ways is a Christian to be a contrast to the people mentioned in verses 3 and 4? (See especially verses 2 and 5.)

6. How did Paul evaluate his life's work (verses 6-8)?

7. When you near the end of your life, what would you like to be able to say about it?

◆ **8.** What were the specific problems Paul was facing in prison?

How did he seek to have those needs met?

9. Paul had had a number of hard experiences and was about to be executed. How then could he say, "The Lord will rescue me from every evil attack"?

10. As a Christian, what is your commission?

In what ways do Paul's encouragements to Timothy help you to fulfill your charge?

Closing Thoughts

Think back over these letters. What impresses you the most about Paul and Timothy's relationship?

What steps can you take to develop a ministry of encouragement to others?

LEADER'S NOTES

■ **Study 1/How Do We Know When We're True to the Truth?**

Question 3. You want each person to think about each objection of Paul's rather than just list his objections. What different kinds of objections does Paul have to these men as teachers? How would you classify these objections? How are some objections similar to each other? How are some different?

Question 12. If your group has trouble identifying some of these ways, you might suggest a few: as a parent, friend, teacher. How, in these capacities, are we to exercise our trust? Do any have a special job? Leave fifteen to twenty minutes of discussion time for these last questions if possible.

■ **Study 2/ How Does God Equip Us for Service?**

Question 8. Hymenaeus and Alexander mentioned in 1 Timothy 1:20 are probably some of the people Paul was thinking of earlier in verses 6 and 7. One of the standard interpretations of the phrase "handed over to Satan," in verse 20, indicates an excommunication from the fellowship for disciplinary purposes.

■ Study 3/ How Can We Live a Tranquil Life?

Question 6. Allow time for each person to write the names of people and a prayer request for each. Don't spend time discussing what you have written. Prayer is, in itself, a meaningful way of sharing. The prayer time is important, but you will need to control the time; that's why it is necessary to stress using "sentence prayers."

Question 8. In the culture to which Paul was writing, braided hair was not pigtails, but an intricately braided style, piled high on top of the head and adorned with jewels. It took hours to produce and was, at the least, distracting, drawing attention to the wearer's wealth and fashion. What are our cultural equivalents?

Question 10. The meaning of 1 Timothy 2:15 is not entirely clear. If it is translated "saved through childbearing," scholars suggest it means that women will be protected in childbirth by continuing in the virtues mentioned. If the phrase is translated "by the birth of the child" (either translation is possible from the original languages), then scholars believe the passage refers to salvation through Jesus Christ who was born of a woman. There is little critical support for an interpretation that only those women who bear children will be saved.

Paul's overriding concern, in this passage as elsewhere, was that the cause of Christ should be promoted and that Christian community life should be stamped with the dignity and order that is evident in the character of God. This series of questions about women is designed to accentuate the positive. It won't be profitable to discuss the negatives (what not to do), or to get into a squabble about whether Paul had an anti-female bias, or to discuss comparative cultures. Help your group use the time to discover the reasons behind Paul's suggestions, so that this discussion may be positive rather than negative.

Study 4/ What Are Requirements for Leaders in God's Household?

Question 2. See also Titus 1:5-7, where Paul identifies elders and overseers, or at least assigns the two offices the same structural rank.

Questions 2-4. Notice the categories these qualifications cover: moral, social, spiritual, intellectual; both attitudes and actions; relationships to the church, outsiders, family, self, possessions. What importance must a job hold that has such sweeping standards? Do we think of these positions as carrying that much weight?

Questions 7-8. These are not the same question. There is a difference between "help its members be ready" and "develop." One has to do with helping church members grow to the point of fitness to be candidates for responsibility, the other with taking people already of this caliber and helping them mature further and become better able to carry out their responsibility.

Question 12. Regarding the prayer time: there is no need for a discussion of needs and problems. It is possible to say "amen" to another's prayer even though the particular situation and individual are not known to everyone. Encourage specific, personal prayer even though the members of your group may come from different churches.

■ Study 5/ How Can I Be a Good Disciple?

Question 2. For other references to questionable rules, see Romans 14 and 1 Corinthians 10:18-33.

Question 6. The phrase in 1 Timothy 4:10, "the Savior of all men, and especially of those who believe" may cause some problems. Colossians 1:17 says that all things hold together because of Jesus Christ. 2 Peter 3:7-9 says God is patiently waiting to judge sin so all may have a chance to repent. All people, therefore, owe their physical lives to God. However, Christians owe their spiritual lives to him as well; he is "especially" the Savior of those who believe.

■ Study 6/ How Are Christians to Care for One Another?

Question 4. God's concern for widows and orphans is evident throughout the Bible. The Old Testament gives clear commands for their provision and condemns those who take advantage of a widow's unprotected position. (See Exodus 22:22-24; Deuteronomy 14:28-29; 24:19-22; and Ruth 2). The New Testament shows the same concern. In Mark 12:40 Jesus condemns Pharisees who look holy but evict widows from their homes, and James 1:27 says that true religion consists in active care for the fatherless and widows.

In these letters to Timothy Paul spells out the church's obligation to protect widows and establishes some regulations that will keep this protection from being misused. These legitimate widows were those who were left all alone without family or means of support. (See Acts 6:1.) They apparently committed themselves to certain responsibilities in the church, almost like a guild, in exchange for provisions such as food and clothing. This arrangement was clearly not "welfare."

Question 11. Today there is somewhat more financial security for widows; jobs for women are more numerous and government aid is sometimes available. However, a widow's life is still a difficult one, and this study should help your group become more alert to these special problems, more aware of God's loving concern, and more responsive to his desire that we express his love toward other Christians facing these problems. Your job as discussion leader is to help your group search the passage for principles of attitude and conduct, and then guide the discussion into specific, practical ways Christians can share God's concern for widows and orphans.

"What about divorcees?" is a question that may be asked by someone. The problems of divorce and widowhood are undoubtedly similar, but there are particular complications posed by the biblical teaching about divorce, and these are not handled by this passage. It is recommended that the discussion be kept to those who are "widows indeed," since that is the group Paul specifies here.

■ Study 7/ How Am I My Brother's Keeper?

Question 6. The laying on of hands is an act by which those in leadership positions commission others, investing them with authority and calling God's blessing upon them.

■ Study 8/ What's So Good about the Good Life?

Question 2. After reading the passage for today, this question takes your group back into the book to trace a theme that has been a persistent one in Paul's letter. Assign different people to read each reference aloud; after each, help your group distinguish the characteristics that apply to the teaching and to the teachers, and then record these in the appropriate space in the studyguide.

Question 3. These false teachers must not be confused with people who ask honest questions or get sidetracked to certain issues as they seek God. Paul is referring to individuals who are actually devious in the way they use religion and people of faith. Sometimes they are not easily recognizable. However, the Holy Spirit will help us to distinguish these people from true seekers.

■ Study 9/ What Reason Do We Have to Be Confident?

Question 2. Since the first letter, Paul had probably paid the visit to Timothy that he had promised (1 Timothy 3:14-15), and had traveled on to Rome where he was imprisoned (2 Timothy 1:16-17). The Christian persecution of Nero's day was in full swing, and the traditional view that Paul was beheaded is more than likely correct. Shortly before his death, then, Paul sent this letter to his young friend Timothy. John Stott comments that it was "also—and consciously— his last will and testament to the church."

Question 8. Since it is difficult to talk about situations in which we have felt shame or fear, it might help to ask one or two people to think about this in advance and be ready to share a particular situation.

■ Study 10/ What Are My Goals?

Question 6. A metaphor is figurative language in which one object is compared to another in order to suggest some likeness between them.

■ Study 11/ How Can We Handle Times of Stress?

Question 9. Jannes and Jambres, mentioned in 2 Timothy 3:8, were two magicians at Pharaoh's court who opposed Moses. Except for this reference they are not mentioned by name in the Bible, but are mentioned in other historical documents.

Study 12/ How Can We Keep Going?

Question 8. Note that Paul looked for help both from other people as well as from the Lord; there is a place for both kinds of help.

WHAT SHOULD WE STUDY NEXT?

To help your group answer that question, we've listed the Fisherman Guides by category so you can choose your next study.

TOPICAL STUDIES

Becoming Women of Purpose, Barton

Building Your House on the Lord, Brestin

Discipleship, Reapsome

Doing Justice, Showing Mercy, Wright

Encouraging Others, Johnson

Examining the Claims of Jesus, Brestin

Friendship, Brestin

Great Doctrines of the Bible, Board

Great Passages of the Bible, Plueddemann

Great People of the Bible, Plueddemann

Great Prayers of the Bible, Plueddemann

Guidance & God's Will, Stark

Higher Ground, Brestin

How Should a Christian Live? (1, 2, & 3 John), Brestin

Let's Pray Together, Fromer & Keyes

Marriage, Stevens

Meeting Jesus, Sire

Moneywise, Larsen

One Body, One Spirit, Larsen

The Parables of Jesus, Hunt

Prayer, Jones

Relationships, Hunt

Satisfying Work, Stevens & Schoberg

Senior Saints, Reapsome

Sermon on the Mount, Hunt

When Servants Suffer, Rhodes

Who Is Jesus?, Van Reken

Worship, Sibley

BIBLE BOOK STUDIES

Genesis, Fromer & Keyes

Psalms, Klug

Proverbs & Parables, Brestin

Ecclesiastes, Brestin

Jonah, Habakkuk, & Malachi, Fromer & Keyes

Matthew, Sibley

Mark, Christensen

Luke, Keyes

John: Living Word, Kuniholm

Acts 1-12, Christensen

Paul (Acts 13-28), Christensen

Romans: Christian Story (basic), Reapsome

Romans: Made Righteous (advanced), Hunt

1 Corinthians, Hummel

Strengthened to Serve (2 Corinthians), Plueddemann

Galatians, Titus & Philemon, Kuniholm

Ephesians, Baylis

Philippians, Klug

Colossians, Shaw

Letters to the Thessalonians, Fromer & Keyes

Letters to Timothy, Fromer & Keyes

Hebrews, Hunt

James, Christensen

1 & 2 Peter, Jude, Brestin

How Should a Christian Live? (1, 2 & 3 John), Brestin

Revelation, Hunt

BIBLE CHARACTER STUDIES

Ruth & Daniel, Stokes

David: Volume 1, Castleman

David: Volume 2, Castleman

Elijah, Castleman

Job, Klug

Men Like Us, Heidebrecht & Scheuermann

Peter, Castleman

Paul (Acts 13-28), Christensen

Great People of the Bible, Plueddemann

Women Like Us, Barton

Women Who Achieved for God, Christensen

Women Who Believed God, Christensen